Through the lens of autism

CWJ Catsanos

Presentation by *BookLeaf Publishing*

Web: www.bookleafpub.com

E-mail: info@bookleafpub.com

ISBN: 9789360947705

First edition 2024

*For all autistic people in the world,
especially those affected by ableism.*

ACKNOWLEDGEMENT

Thanks to all the wonderful autistic people in my life and all the wonderful therapists who have helped me to become the man I am today.

My value

What shall my value be?
Is it in my neurodiversity?
Am I not normal? Is it that my worth
Is less than most on earth?

The ableist lies I hear
Become the whisperings of my inner ear,
And I this ableism internalise,
And tell myself these lies.

No! This is my true worth:
The same as all who live upon the earth;
No-one can tell me that I'm second-best,
Or worth less than the rest.

Let me my value see,
Within my great neurodiversity;
For I am just as worthy as are you,
I know this to be true.

Communication

When people use their words,
Their meaning is made known;
And in the language that I hear,
Their will to me is shown.

But often what they say
Is not what's in their heart,
And they a different meaning bring,
And something else impart.

No wonder I'm confused
When they see me misled;
But no, I'm not the problem here,
I did all that they said!

Don't play around with words!
I hear them as they sound,
And I will do just as they say,
And will not fool around!

Distractions

They ask me if I heard them,
Or noticed what they said;
But so much extra data
Is rolling in my head!
I have no time to process
The wealth of data here;
So it is little wonder
That I don't always hear!

I wonder how they'd take it
If they, as much as I,
Had so much extra data
That all their brains supply!
It takes a lot of thinking
To put it all aside,
Therefore if I'm distracted,
Just take it in your stride!

(The fact which is the inspiration of this poem, is that the autistic brain can generate up to 42% more data than the neurotypical brain, which is a common cause of distraction in autistic individuals in day-to-day life. It is not to imply that neurotypicals are not as intelligent as autistics.)

Don't tidy after me

My space may seem disorganised,
But I see otherwise;
What you may see as piles of mess
Are treasures in my eyes!
I know where everything is kept
And what I need to do;
This is my space, it's sweet to me,
Even if not to you.

My brain is not the same as yours,
So don't make me conform
To your idea of organised,
Which isn't quite my form!
I know it may peculiar look,
In what you here may see;
But it's my space, and it is safe:
Don't tidy after me!

Showing love

I am a loving person,
I know this to be true;
But I, in how I show my love,
Am not the same as you.
Sometimes, I'll share a message
Which brought into my heart
A thought of you and what you love,
Thus I my love impart.

It may be in an action
Designed to help you out;
It may be when I sit by you
Whene'er you scream or shout.
It may be in a gesture,
A simple hug or kiss,
Something which I don't freely share,
But which you sorely miss.

So don't think I'm not loving,
Because the way I show
Is different from most other folk,
Different from what you know.
Please know I really love you,
Please know I really care,
While others may not see my love,
Please know that it is there.

Special interests

When I have a special interest,
It can go right to my heart;
And with you I want to share it,
Hoping to my joy impart.

Sometimes, though, you cannot see it,
Sometimes, though, it seems a bore;
Maybe you don't see its value,
Even I may seem a chore.

But, please know that in my sharing
Is a wish to make you glad;
For without my special interest
My life would be very sad!

Over-explaining

When I tell you something,
I like to explain it,
Because I am frightened
You won't understand;
But when I explain it,
I go into detail,
More detail, and detail,
Much more than I planned.
It's not that I'm stupid,
It's not that you're stupid,
It's just that your speaking
Is different from mine;
So when I explain it,
Explain and explain it,
I make sure you get me,
And that's where I shine!

My good things

I am a gentle soul,
And I'm an old soul, too;
Yes, I can be a comfort when
I interact with you!

When I an interest find,
I can be very good,
And this is great, though some may think
I know more than I should.

My thinking can be deep;
This shows you that I care;
Though you don't always see my love,
I know that it is there.

And if you should be blessed
To have me as a friend,
You'll know I'm genuine and safe,
And with you to the end.

Burnout

I work so hard to be someone
Who lives a "normal" life;
But sometimes this can be too much
And put my brain in strife!
For though I do the best I can,
There still can be no doubt
That all the things I try to hide
At times may burn me out!

But when I do burn out, please know
That I have really tried
To do the best in all I do,
And my deep pain to hide;
Please be as patient as you can,
There's nothing I can do
To stop myself from burning out:
Just think if it were you!

But why?

It's hard to just accept
That something has to be:
I always have to know: "But why?"
That's just a part of me!

Sometimes it will make sense;
Sometimes it will confuse;
So if I need to know: "But why?"
Please don't me this refuse!

It's just that I can't work
With something I don't know;
So please, if I just ask "But why?"
Your reasons to me show!

I'm grateful that you can
Help me to see your way;
I'm grateful, if I ask "But why?"
For all things that you say.

Dysregulation

Sometimes all my function
Goes into confusion;
This dysregulation
Is part of my day.
There's nothing to fix it,
It doesn't need fixing,
It's just in my thinking,
For I am this way.
Just let me take rest breaks,
And don't overwhelm me;
A break from deep thinking
Is all that I need.
It's part of my brain style,
It's part of my thinking;
Please hear what I tell you,
And all my cues heed.

Boundaries

Please listen to my boundaries,
And show me true respect;
Just as you'd ask of others,
To decency reflect.
I too am still a human,
I feel and think like you;
So what you'd want from others,
The same to me please do.

Just 'cause I am autistic
Does not make me a child;
So treat me like an adult,
And don't think this is wild!
I live and work like you do,
I have no lesser worth;
I'm worth the same as all folk
Who live upon the earth.

But you don't look autistic!

What does autistic look like?
Does it not look like me?
I don't know what you look at,
I don't know what you see.
But autism has not one size,
It shows in many ways;
If I don't look autistic,
The problem is your gaze.

For autism is a spectrum
As wide as all the sea;
And right there on the spectrum
Is such a soul as me!
I am, as much as others
Who on the spectrum lie,
A true autistic person,
It's my identity.

If I don't look autistic,
Then think, and think it through;
I do not fake my autism;
The problem, then, is you.
I wish you'd see my autism
As plainly as do I;
There's no one look of autism
Perceived by human eye.

Patterns

The patterns that I daily see,
In numbers, one and two and three,
In letters, shapes and other ways,
Give added brightness to my days.

I may not see the things you do;
But I see patterns through and through!
While these may pass most others by,
They're never missed by my keen eye.

Sometimes these patterns don't do much;
They're there, but aren't a help as such.
But sometimes do these patterns hold,
New knowledge; treasures manifold.

So when I see these patterns, know
That maybe to the world I'll show
A wealth of opportunity,
In my neurodiversity.

Masking

Sometimes I need to mask,
So "normal" I appear;
But masking is not good for me,
It is a dreaded fear.

For when I mask myself,
To be someone I'm not,
The value that's in all I am
Can often be forgot.

And being who I'm not
Exhausts me through and through;
I then forget what I can say,
And all that I can do.

Don't make me mask myself!
Just like you show your face,
Let my autistic life shine through,
Let me myself embrace!

I love you

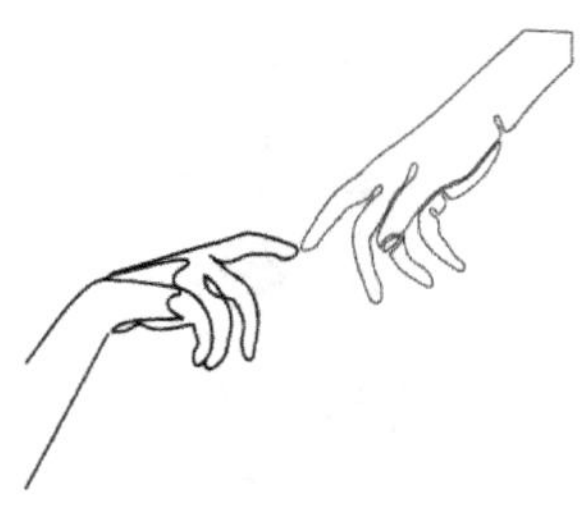

"I love you"!
Believe this to be true!
I may not show love like you do,
But I love you!

"I love you"!
I need to feel at peace,
Before I kiss you, or embrace,
But I love you!

"I love you"!
I may not like to talk,
I may with you in silence walk,
But I love you!

"I love you"!
I may not always prove,
I may show different forms of love,
But I love you!

My special life

My life may look different,
It's not what you're used to;
I have different hobbies,
I do different things.
But my life is special,
It is what I've made it,
And it is fulfilling;
I live it on wings!
It has all its good times,
It has all its bad times,
It has all its wonders,
It has all its strife;
But it's what I make it,
For I am autistic,
And I'm happy with it,
For it is my life!

Autism

What is autism?
It is the truth of who I am,
It is my pride, it is no shame.
That is autism!

What is autism?
It is a gift which I embrace,
It is my joy and happy place,
That is autism!

What is autism?
It is the wonder of my life,
My happiness in woes and strife,
That is autism!

What is autism?
It is my favourite way to be,
It is my life, and it is me,
That is autism!